Welcome to 21 L &

Congratulations on taking this first step toward a transformative journey with God! This devotional guide is designed to lead you through 21 days of spiritual growth, renewed clarity, and strengthened confidence in your walk with Christ. Each day will draw you closer to living a life fully aligned with God's promises and purpose, equipping you with the tools to integrate faith into every aspect of your life.

At its core, this guide is about cultivating a holistic approach to life—honoring your mind, body, and spirit in ways that reflect God's truth and align with His plan for you. Throughout these 21 days, you'll explore key concepts like embracing a growth mindset, trusting God's timing, and building sustainable habits for spiritual, emotional, and mental growth.

This is not just a daily task to check off but an intentional journey toward deeper faith and self-discovery. You'll reflect on scripture, engage with meaningful prompts, and apply practical steps to grow in alignment with God's will. Each day builds upon the last, creating a foundation of faith that will continue to support you long after these 21 days have ended.

What to Expect

This devotional guide is thoughtfully structured to help you:

- Discover Holistic Living: Align your mind, body, and spirit with God's purpose.
- Develop a Growth Mindset: Transform how you see challenges by trusting God to renew your thoughts and actions.
- Build Sustainable Faith Habits: Establish routines and practices that deepen your connection to God and sustain long-term growth.
- Strengthen Your Confidence in God: Learn to trust His timing, guidance, and promises in every aspect of your life.

Each day includes:

- Scripture to anchor your reflections and set the tone for your day.
- A Reflection to inspire and challenge you to think more deeply about your faith.
- Guided Prompts to help you connect the daily themes to your personal journey.
- Practical Steps to apply what you've learned and move closer to God's plan.
- Prayer to center your heart and align your actions with His will.

Suggestions for the Journey

- Start Each Morning with God: Dedicate 15-30 minutes to begin your day with scripture, reflection, and prayer. Let this guide shape your mindset and set a positive tone for the day.
- Reflect in the Evening: Before ending your day, take time to revisit the day's prompts and reflect on how God has been present in your actions and thoughts.
- Be Consistent: Transformation happens through intentionality and consistency. Set a routine and protect your time with God.
- Pause for Weekly Reflection: At the end of each week, take advantage of the reflection pages to celebrate your progress, identify areas for growth, and prepare for the week ahead.
- Pray Through the Process: Invite God into every step of your journey. Ask for clarity, strength, and wisdom as you grow deeper in faith.

A Journey Toward Alignment with God's Purpose

As you embark on these 21 days, know that this guide was created with a deep desire to help you experience the fullness of God's promises. It's a journey not just of learning but of transformation—a chance to walk closer with Him, to see His hand in every area of your life, and to trust that His plans are good.

Let this guide inspire you to embrace holistic living, develop a renewed mindset, and grow in faith and confidence as you align with God's purpose. This is your time to start living fully, deeply, and intentionally in the light of His promises.

Are you ready to begin? Let's take the first step together.

Day 1
Understanding Holistic Living

"I came that they may have life and have it abundantly."

– John 10:10

God's design for our lives is one of abundance—not just in material wealth, but in the richness of our spiritual, mental, and physical well-being. Holistic living reflects this divine plan by aligning every part of our lives with His purpose. This means understanding that our faith is not limited to Sunday services or specific moments of prayer, but should flow into how we treat our bodies, nurture our minds, and connect with others.

Holistic living invites us to ask:
- Are we feeding our spirit with the Word of God daily?
- Are we taking care of our bodies as the temples God created?
- Are we pursuing a mindset of gratitude and trust rather than fear and anxiety?

By aligning all aspects of our life with God's will, we create space for Him to work through us. Holistic living doesn't mean perfection—it means surrender. It's recognizing that every part of our being is interconnected and that God wants us to live joyfully and purposefully in all areas.

As you move through this day, reflect on what it means to live holistically. Let this be a reminder that God is present in the smallest and largest parts of your life. This day is an opportunity to start seeing every moment, choice, and thought as a reflection of His love for you.

Intention Setting
Today, focus on inviting God into all areas of your life:
1. Mind: Reflect on what thoughts bring you closer to God and what thoughts distract you.
2. Body: Honor your body through small, caring actions like drinking water, taking a walk, or resting.
3. Spirit: Dedicate time to prayer or scripture to strengthen your connection with God.

Gratitude Focus
Today, focus on recognizing God's goodness in:
1. A small joy: Did someone smile at you? Did you hear a song that lifted your heart?
2. God's creation: Notice the beauty of the world around you—a sunrise, a flower, or the sound of birds.
3. A moment of peace: Did you experience a moment today where you felt calm and grounded?

Action Plan
1. Morning Mindfulness: Spend 5 minutes in prayer or quiet reflection, asking God to guide your thoughts.
2. Caring for Your Body: Choose one action to honor your physical well-being—drink a glass of water, eat a nourishing meal, or take a short walk.
3. Evening Reflection: At the end of the day, think about how you saw God working in your life and how you honored Him through your actions.

Prayer for Holistic Living
Heavenly Father,

Thank You for creating me as a whole person—mind, body, and spirit. Help me to see the ways You are working in every part of my life. Teach me to honor You through my thoughts, my actions, and my faith. Let my life reflect Your abundance and purpose, and guide me to live holistically, fully aligned with Your will. Amen.

Day 2
Developing a Growth Mindset

"Do not be conformed to this world, but be transformed by the renewal of your mind." — Romans 12:2

A growth mindset is the belief that you can grow, change, and improve through effort and God's guidance. Romans 12:2 reminds us that transformation begins in the mind. When we align our thoughts with God's truth, we open ourselves to His abundant grace and possibilities.

God calls us to let go of worldly patterns of thinking—fear, doubt, and negativity—and instead embrace His promises of renewal. Developing a growth mindset doesn't mean avoiding challenges; it means viewing them as opportunities to grow in faith and resilience.

Each day offers a chance to trust God more deeply and believe in His ability to work through us. With a growth mindset, we can see failures as lessons, obstacles as opportunities, and struggles as reminders of God's strength working in our weakness.

Today, reflect on areas where you may feel limited by fear or doubt. Ask God to help you replace those thoughts with His truth and renew your perspective. Transformation begins with a single thought aligned with His will.

Intention Setting
Today, focus on these three intentions as you cultivate a growth mindset:
1. Identify a Limiting Belief: Reflect on one thought or habit that keeps you from living in alignment with God's truth.
2. Practice Positivity: Replace discouragement with a scripture or affirmation, such as "I am fearfully and wonderfully made" (Psalm 139:14).
3. Move Toward Renewal: Take one intentional step to break free from old patterns of thinking.

Gratitude Focus
Today, let gratitude shape your growth as you reflect on:
1. A lesson you've learned through a recent challenge. What did God teach you that helped you grow?
2. An area of your life where you've seen progress. What has improved as you trusted God?
3. The people who inspire or encourage you. How has God used others to guide you forward?

Action Plan
Transformation requires intentional steps. Today, commit to:
1. Revisiting Scripture: Write Romans 12:2 somewhere visible (like your mirror or phone) as a daily reminder to renew your mind.
2. Stepping Outside Your Comfort Zone: Identify one task or decision you've been avoiding and take a small step toward completing it.
3. Evaluating Your Environment: Look at your physical or mental surroundings and make one change that supports a growth mindset (e.g., decluttering, creating a prayer space, or limiting distractions).

Prayer for a Growth Mindset
Heavenly Father,

Thank You for the power of renewal. Teach me to surrender my thoughts and patterns to You so that I may be transformed by Your truth. Help me to embrace challenges as opportunities to grow closer to You and to trust Your promises in every situation. Show me how to align my actions, thoughts, and habits with Your will so I can walk in the purpose You've prepared for me.

Amen.

Day 3
Aligning Goals with Faith

"Commit your work to the Lord, and your plans will be established." — Proverbs 16:3

Aligning our goals with faith means surrendering our desires to God and inviting Him to guide our path. Proverbs 16:3 reminds us that when we commit our work to the Lord, He establishes our plans. This isn't about asking God to bless our ambitions but about seeking His will above our own.

Goals rooted in faith come with clarity and peace because they align with God's greater plan for our lives. Sometimes, this means letting go of what we think we want to make room for what God knows we need. Other times, it means trusting His timing, even when the results don't come as quickly as we hope.

As we align our goals with faith, we must examine the motives behind them. Are our goals meant to glorify God, or do they come from a place of fear, pride, or comparison? By bringing our ambitions into the light of God's Word, we can discern which ones align with His purpose and which ones need to be redefined or released.

This process of alignment requires trust and surrender. Trust that God knows what's best for us and surrender the need to control every outcome. It's not always easy, but it leads to a deeper connection with Him and a greater sense of purpose in our daily lives.

Today, reflect on your goals. Ask yourself which ones feel aligned with God's will and which ones need to be reexamined. Invite Him into your plans, trusting that He will establish them according to His wisdom and love.

Intention Setting
Today, focus on aligning your goals with God's will:
1. Reassess Your Goals: Identify one goal and reflect on its alignment with God's purpose.
2. Invite God into Your Plans: Dedicate your daily tasks to Him and trust His guidance.
3. Release Control: Let go of the need to control outcomes and trust God's timing.

Gratitude Focus
Today, reflect on God's goodness in:
1. A goal you've achieved with His help.
2. Opportunities He's given you to grow.
3. God's guidance when plans didn't work out as expected.

Action Plan
Take intentional steps to align your goals with faith:
1. Write Down a Goal: Choose one specific goal and commit it to prayer, asking for God's guidance.
2. Break It Down: Identify small, manageable steps you can take today and dedicate those steps to God.
3. Reflect at Day's End: Consider how surrendering your plans to God brought clarity or peace to your day.

Prayer for Aligning Goals with Faith
Heavenly Father,

Help me to align my goals with Your will. Teach me to release my plans into Your hands and to trust Your guidance in all things. May my ambitions reflect Your purpose and bring glory to Your name. Remind me that true success comes from walking in faith and trusting Your path. Amen.

Day 4
Removing Spiritual Obstacles

"Therefore, since we are surrounded by so great a cloud of witnesses, let us also lay aside every weight, and sin which clings so closely, and let us run with endurance the race that is set before us." – Hebrews 12:1

Transformation with God requires us to examine the weights that hold us back. Hebrews 12:1 calls us to lay aside anything that hinders our ability to run the race He has set before us.

These weights may appear in the form of sinful habits, unhealthy relationships, unresolved bitterness, or even a lack of faith in God's promises.

Sometimes, these obstacles feel too heavy to release on our own, but God is always ready to help us. By bringing these weights to Him in prayer, we allow His strength to replace our weakness. Identifying and removing these obstacles is not about judgment or shame; it's about clearing the path so we can move forward in freedom and grace.

Today, reflect on areas in your life where you feel burdened or stuck. Ask God to reveal the spiritual weights that need to be removed and to provide the courage and strength to release them. Transformation begins when we let go of what no longer serves His purpose and trust Him to guide us toward the abundant life He has promised.

Intention Setting
Today, focus on identifying and removing spiritual obstacles:
1. Recognize your weights. Ask God to reveal anything in your life that may be hindering your walk with Him.
2. Release burdens to God. Pray for the courage to let go of these obstacles and surrender them into God's hands.
3. Embrace freedom in Christ. Walk confidently, knowing that God's grace covers you and empowers you to move forward.

Gratitude Focus
Today, reflect on God's goodness in:
1. The freedom He provides from burdens.
2. Moments when He has carried you through challenges.
3. His endless grace and patience as you grow.

Action Plan
Take steps to release spiritual obstacles and embrace God's freedom:
1. Identify a specific weight. Spend time in prayer asking God to reveal one area in your life that is holding you back.
2. Take a step toward release. Write a note of surrender to God or take a physical action (e.g., removing a negative influence, forgiving someone, or creating space for prayer).
3. Reflect on the process. At the end of the day, think about how letting go of this burden allowed you to move closer to God's purpose.

Prayer for Removing Spiritual Obstacles
Heavenly Father,

Thank You for calling me to run the race You have set before me. Reveal the weights and sins that are holding me back and give me the courage to release them into Your hands. Help me to trust in Your strength to carry what I cannot. Let Your grace empower me to move forward, free from burdens, and fully aligned with Your will. Amen.

Day 5
Surrendering to God's Plans

"For I know the plans I have for you, declares the Lord, plans for welfare and not for evil, to give you a future and a hope." – Jeremiah 29:11

Surrendering to God's plans means trusting Him with every detail of our lives. Jeremiah 29:11 reminds us that God's plans are always good, even when we can't see the full picture. While we may try to control our circumstances or cling to our own desires, true transformation comes when we release that control and allow God to lead.

Surrender is not a sign of weakness—it is an act of faith. It means believing that God's wisdom surpasses our understanding and trusting Him to guide us toward the future He has prepared. This process often requires patience and letting go of what feels comfortable or familiar.

Today, reflect on areas where you struggle to let go and invite God into those places. Ask Him to replace your doubts with faith, your fear with peace, and your plans with His perfect purpose. Surrender is the key to unlocking the abundant life He promises.

Intention Setting
Today, focus on surrendering to God's plans:
1. Identify areas of resistance. Ask God to show you where you are holding on too tightly to your own plans.
2. Trust in His wisdom. Reflect on Jeremiah 29:11 and remind yourself that His plans are for your good.
3. Commit to letting go. Take one step toward releasing control and trusting God to lead.

Gratitude Focus
Today, reflect on God's goodness in:
1. The ways He has guided you in the past.
2. The peace that comes from trusting Him.
3. His promise to give you a future filled with hope.

Action Plan
Take practical steps to surrender your plans to God:
1. Write down one area of your life where you need to let go. Pray specifically for God's guidance and strength to release control.
2. Take one action that demonstrates your trust in God, such as saying "yes" to an opportunity outside your comfort zone or forgiving someone who has hurt you.
3. Reflect at the end of the day on how surrendering to God's plans brought clarity or peace.

Prayer for Surrendering to God's Plans
Heavenly Father,

Thank You for the plans You have for me, plans that are good and full of hope. Help me to surrender my desires and trust in Your perfect wisdom. Replace my fears with faith and my doubts with peace. Lead me in the path You have prepared, and let my life reflect Your purpose and glory. Amen.

Day 6
Walking in Newness of Life

"Therefore, if anyone is in Christ, he is a new creation. The old has passed away; behold, the new has come." – 2 Corinthians 5:17

Through Christ, we are made new. When we accept Him as our Savior, we leave behind the weight of our old lives—sins, regrets, and past mistakes—and step into the newness of life that He offers. 2 Corinthians 5:17 reminds us that transformation isn't just a surface change; it's a complete renewal of who we are, rooted in God's grace.

Walking in newness of life means living in alignment with our new identity in Christ. It's about seeing ourselves through God's eyes—redeemed, loved, and purposed. However, it also requires intentionality. Old habits and thoughts may try to pull us back, but through prayer and dependence on the Holy Spirit, we can walk confidently in the freedom Christ has given us.

Today, reflect on what it means to live as a new creation. What parts of your old life need to be left behind? What areas of your life need to be renewed in Christ? Embrace this newness and let it guide your actions, thoughts, and interactions with others.

Intention Setting
Today, focus on living as a new creation in Christ:
1. Release old habits. Identify one habit or mindset that no longer aligns with your identity in Christ.
2. Embrace your new identity. Reflect on who God says you are: loved, redeemed, and purposed.
3. Walk in freedom. Take a step of faith today that reflects the newness of life you have in Christ.

Gratitude Focus
Today, reflect on God's goodness in:
1. The gift of a fresh start through Christ.
2. The freedom to leave the past behind.
3. The guidance of the Holy Spirit in your daily walk.

Action Plan
Take practical steps to live as a new creation:
1. Write down one area of your life where you feel stuck in the past. Pray for God to renew this area and help you move forward.
2. Take an action that reflects your new identity in Christ, such as offering forgiveness, showing kindness, or choosing faith over fear.
3. Reflect at the end of the day on how walking in newness of life impacted your actions and mindset.

Prayer for Walking in Newness of Life
Heavenly Father,

Thank You for making me a new creation in Christ. Help me to leave behind the old and embrace the freedom and purpose You have given me. Renew my heart, my thoughts, and my actions so that they reflect my identity in You. Guide me each day as I walk in the newness of life You have provided through Your Son. Amen.

Day 7
Trusting in God's Timing

"He has made everything beautiful in its time." – Ecclesiastes 3:11

Trusting in God's timing requires faith and patience. Ecclesiastes 3:11 reminds us that God's plans unfold in perfect timing, even when we can't see or understand the full picture. It's often challenging to wait on God when we're eager for change or resolution, but His timing is always purposeful and intentional.

In a world that values instant gratification, waiting on God can feel counterintuitive. Yet, His timing is never rushed or delayed. He sees the beginning and the end of every situation and knows the exact moment to act for our good and His glory. Trusting in His timing means believing that He is always at work, even in seasons of waiting.

Consider the beauty of God's creation: flowers bloom in their season, rivers flow at their pace, and the sun rises and sets each day. These natural rhythms are reminders of God's order and care. Similarly, our lives are part of His divine rhythm, and when we align with His timing, we experience the peace and fulfillment that only He can provide.

Today, reflect on an area where you feel impatient or unsure. Ask God to teach you to trust in His timing and to see His hand at work in your life. Waiting on Him is not a passive act; it's an opportunity to grow in faith and prepare for the beauty He is orchestrating in your life.

Intention Setting
Today, focus on trusting God's timing:
1. Identify a situation where you feel impatient. Surrender it to God and ask Him to guide your perspective.
2. Seek God's peace. Reflect on Ecclesiastes 3:11 and trust that He is making everything beautiful in His time.
3. Practice patience. Take one step today to wait with faith, knowing that God's plans are always good.

Gratitude Focus
Today, reflect on God's goodness in:
1. The moments of growth you've experienced during times of waiting.
2. The way God's timing has worked out for your good in the past.
3. The assurance that He is always working behind the scenes.

Action Plan
Take practical steps to align with God's timing:
1. Pause and pray. When you feel impatient or frustrated, take a moment to pray for God's peace and guidance.
2. Celebrate the present. Identify one blessing or opportunity you might overlook while waiting for what's next.
3. Reflect at the end of the day. Think about how practicing patience and trusting in God's timing impacted your mindset and actions.

Prayer for Trusting in God's Timing
Heavenly Father,

Thank You for orchestrating every moment of my life with care and intention. Teach me to trust in Your perfect timing, even when I feel impatient or uncertain. Help me to see the beauty in the present and to have faith that You are working all things together for good. Replace my anxiety with peace and my doubt with trust as I wait on You. Amen.

Week 1 Reflection

1. What have you learned about yourself during this week?

2. How has your relationship with God deepened?

3. What challenges did you face, and how did you overcome them?

4. What moments of growth or breakthroughs did you experience?

Week 1 Assessment

1. What areas of your life still need attention or surrender to God?

2. How have your habits or mindset shifted during Week 1?

3. What specific goals or intentions will you carry into Week 2?

4. How can you rely on God's strength to continue your transformation?

Day 8
Building a Firm Foundation

Everyone then who hears these words of mine and does them will be like a wise man who built his house on the rock. — Matthew 7:24

Transformation is built on a solid foundation, and Matthew 7:24 reminds us that this foundation is God's Word. When we root our lives in His truth, we gain the stability to withstand challenges and grow in His purpose. A firm foundation is not just about hearing His Word but also about applying it daily in our decisions, thoughts, and actions.

Think of a house built on sand versus one built on rock. When storms come, the house on sand collapses because it lacks a sturdy foundation. Similarly, without God's Word anchoring us, we can easily be swept away by life's uncertainties, doubts, and trials.

Building a firm foundation requires intentional effort. It means prioritizing time with God, meditating on His promises, and allowing His truth to shape every area of your life. As you grow in faith, you'll notice that the storms of life may come, but they won't shake your confidence in God's plan.

Today, reflect on the foundation of your life. Are you firmly rooted in God's Word, or are there areas where you're relying on unstable ground? Ask God to strengthen your faith and guide you in building a life that stands firm on His truth.

Intention Setting
Today, focus on strengthening your foundation:
1. Reflect on one area of your life where you feel uncertain or unstable. Commit this to God in prayer.
2. Seek stability through Scripture. Meditate on Matthew 7:24 and its meaning for your daily life.
3. Take one small step to apply God's Word in a decision, thought, or action today.

Gratitude Focus
Today, reflect on God's goodness in:
1. The unchanging truth of His Word.
2. His presence during life's storms.
3. The peace that comes from standing on a firm foundation.

Action Plan
Take practical steps to build your foundation:
1. Spend 10 minutes reading and meditating on a Scripture passage that speaks to your current season.
2. Identify one way to replace doubt or instability with trust in God's promises.
3. Reflect at the end of the day on how standing on God's Word brought clarity or peace.

Prayer for Building a Firm Foundation
Heavenly Father,

Thank You for being my unshakable foundation. Help me to root my life in Your Word and to stand firm in the face of challenges. Teach me to apply Your truth daily in my thoughts, decisions, and actions. Strengthen my faith and remind me that with You as my foundation, I can withstand anything. Thank You for being my rock and my refuge. Amen.

Day 9
Overcoming Fear with Faith

For God gave us a spirit not of fear but of power and love and self-control. — 2 Timothy 1:7

Fear is one of the greatest obstacles to faith. It clouds our judgment, weakens our resolve, and distances us from God's promises. Yet 2 Timothy 1:7 reminds us that fear is not from God. Instead, He gives us a spirit of power, love, and self-control to face life's challenges with confidence.

Overcoming fear begins with acknowledging its source. Often, fear arises from the unknown or from placing trust in ourselves rather than in God. But God equips us to confront fear by giving us His strength. His power emboldens us, His love drives out fear, and His self-control anchors us when panic threatens to take hold.

Today, consider where fear has taken root in your life. Is it holding you back from stepping into your purpose? Is it keeping you from trusting God fully? Ask God to reveal His power and love in those areas, and take a small step forward in faith. As you let go of fear, you'll make room for God's peace and strength to fill your heart.

Intention Setting

Today, focus on overcoming fear with faith:
1. Reflect on an area of your life where fear has kept you from trusting God fully.
2. Meditate on 2 Timothy 1:7, declaring His spirit of power, love, and self-control over your life.
3. Take one bold step today to act in faith, even in the face of fear.

Gratitude Focus

Today, reflect on God's goodness in:
1. The power He gives to face challenges.
2. The love that drives out fear.
3. The peace that comes from trusting in His promises.

Action Plan

Take practical steps to overcome fear:
1. Write down one fear you are ready to surrender to God.
2. Pray for God's strength and love to replace that fear.
3. At the end of the day, reflect on how stepping out in faith strengthened your confidence in Him.

Prayer for Overcoming Fear with Faith

Heavenly Father,

Thank You for the spirit of power, love, and self-control that You have given me. Teach me to let go of fear and to trust in Your strength and promises. Replace my doubts with confidence in Your plan, and help me to walk boldly in faith. Thank You for being my refuge and my source of peace. Amen.

DAY 10
Embracing God's Peace

"Peace I leave with you; my peace I give to you. Not as the world gives do I give to you. Let not your hearts be troubled, neither let them be afraid." – John 14:27

The peace God offers is unlike anything the world can provide. While worldly peace often depends on external circumstances—like calm moments or resolved conflicts—God's peace is internal, steadfast, and rooted in His presence. John 14:27 reminds us that Jesus left us His peace, a gift that calms troubled hearts and silences fear.

When we rely solely on worldly solutions, our peace can easily crumble under pressure. But God's peace surpasses understanding; it anchors us even in the midst of chaos. Embracing His peace requires trusting in His sovereignty, believing that He is in control even when life feels uncertain.

Think about areas in your life where you've been searching for peace. Have you looked to temporary fixes or distractions instead of seeking the eternal peace that comes from God? Today is an opportunity to shift your focus. Instead of striving for control, rest in God's promises and let His peace fill your heart.

Intention Setting
Today, focus on embracing God's peace:
1. Reflect on one area of your life where you feel anxious or unsettled. Commit this to God in prayer.
2. Meditate on John 14:27, allowing His peace to quiet your thoughts.
3. Take one small action to cultivate peace today, such as practicing stillness or releasing a worry to God.

Gratitude Focus
Today, reflect on God's goodness in:
1. The unshakable peace He provides in every season.
2. His presence, which calms troubled hearts.
3. The assurance that He is in control, even in uncertain times.

Action Plan
Take practical steps to embrace God's peace:
1. Spend 10 minutes in quiet reflection, inviting God's peace into your heart.
2. Identify one worry or burden to release to Him today.
3. Reflect at the end of the day on how resting in His peace impacted your thoughts and actions.

Prayer for Embracing God's Peace

Heavenly Father,

Thank You for the gift of Your peace, which surpasses all understanding. Teach me to rest in Your presence and to trust in Your sovereignty. Quiet the anxieties in my heart and fill me with the peace that only You can provide. Help me to embrace Your promises and walk in confidence, knowing You are always with me. Amen.

Day 11
Building Resilience

I can do all things through Him who strengthens me. — Philippians 4:13

Resilience is the ability to endure challenges and grow stronger through them. Philippians 4:13 reminds us that we don't face difficulties alone—God strengthens us to persevere and overcome. Resilience is not about avoiding hardships but about trusting God to guide us through them, emerging with greater faith and wisdom.

Think about a time in your life when you faced overwhelming circumstances. What kept you going? Often, it is God's strength, working through us, that enables us to endure when we feel like giving up. Building resilience means leaning on God, trusting His promises, and allowing Him to shape us through trials.

Challenges are opportunities for growth, and resilience develops when we rely on God to turn difficulties into lessons of faith. Today, reflect on how God's strength has carried you through past seasons of hardship. Trust that He will continue to equip you with everything you need to persevere and thrive.

Intention Setting
Today, focus on building resilience:
 1. Reflect on a challenge you're currently facing and commit it to God in prayer.
 2. Meditate on Philippians 4:13, trusting that God will give you the strength to persevere.
 3. Take one action today to rely on God's power instead of your own.

Gratitude Focus
Today, reflect on God's goodness in:
 1. The strength He provides during difficult seasons.
 2. His faithfulness in carrying you through past challenges.
 3. The opportunities for growth that hardships create.

Action Plan
Take practical steps to build resilience:
 1. Write down one way God has strengthened you during a difficult time.
 2. Identify one current challenge and pray for God's guidance to overcome it.
 3. Reflect at the end of the day on how trusting in God's strength helped you persevere.

Prayer for Building Resilience
Heavenly Father,

Thank You for the strength You provide in every season. Teach me to rely on You during hardships and to trust that You are working all things for my good. Help me to grow stronger in faith and character as I face challenges with Your guidance. Thank You for equipping me to persevere and for being my constant source of hope and strength. Amen.

Day 12
Walking in Faithful Obedience

"If you are willing and obedient, you shall eat the good of the land." — Isaiah 1:19

Faithful obedience is the key to experiencing the fullness of God's blessings. Isaiah 1:19 reminds us that willingness and obedience lead to "the good of the land," symbolizing God's provision and favor. Walking in obedience requires trust—believing that God's commands are for our good, even when they challenge our comfort or understanding.

Obedience is not just about following rules; it's about aligning our hearts with God's will and taking action on what He has called us to do. This might mean letting go of something that distracts us from Him, stepping into a new opportunity, or simply trusting Him in a difficult season.

Think of obedience as an act of faith. It says, "God, I trust that Your way is better than mine." When we walk in obedience, we open the door for God to work in and through us. It's not always easy, but it is always rewarding.

Today, consider an area where you've been hesitant to obey God. What step of obedience can you take today to draw closer to His purpose for your life?

Intention Setting
Today, focus on walking in faithful obedience:
1. Reflect on an area where you've been resisting God's direction.
2. Ask God to give you the courage to take a step of obedience, no matter how small.
3. Commit to following through on one specific act of obedience today.

Gratitude Focus
Today, reflect on God's goodness in:
1. The guidance He provides through His Word and Spirit.
2. The blessings that come from aligning with His will.
3. The peace that follows faithful obedience.

Action Plan
Take practical steps to walk in obedience:
1. Write down one area where God is calling you to obey Him.
2. Take one action today that reflects obedience to His call.
3. Reflect at the end of the day on how stepping into obedience strengthened your faith.

Prayer for Faithful Obedience
Heavenly Father,

Thank You for leading me with love and wisdom. Help me to trust Your plan and to walk in faithful obedience to Your will. Give me the courage to take action, even when it feels challenging or uncertain. Teach me to delight in Your commands and to follow You wholeheartedly. Thank You for the blessings that come from obedience and for drawing me closer to You each day. Amen.

Day 13
Discovering Your Purpose

For I know the plans I have for you, declares the Lord. – Jeremiah 29:11

God has a unique purpose for each of us, and Jeremiah 29:11 assures us that His plans are filled with hope and promise. While the journey to discovering your purpose can feel uncertain, it is rooted in seeking God's guidance and trusting His timing. His purpose for you is not about personal gain but about aligning your life with His will and contributing to His kingdom.

Reflect on your gifts, passions, and experiences—these are often clues to the purpose God has placed in your heart. What comes naturally to you? What brings you joy and fulfillment? God uses the unique combination of your talents and life experiences to further His work. However, discovering this purpose requires patience and a willingness to trust Him, even when the path ahead feels unclear.

Today, take time to ask God to reveal the next step in His plan for you. Embrace the process of discovery, knowing that His purpose for you is good, filled with hope, and perfectly timed.

Intention Setting
Today, focus on discovering your purpose:
 1. Reflect on one gift or passion that God has placed in your life.
 2. Ask God to show you how this gift aligns with His plan for you.
 3. Commit to taking one small step toward exploring your God-given purpose.

Gratitude Focus
Today, reflect on God's goodness in:
 1. The unique gifts and passions He has given you.
 2. His plans, which are always good and filled with hope.
 3. The assurance that He is working for your welfare and future.

Action Plan
Take practical steps to discover your purpose:
 1. Write down one passion or talent you feel God has given you.
 2. Identify one way you can use this gift to serve others or further God's kingdom.
 3. Reflect at the end of the day on how exploring your purpose brought clarity or inspiration.

Prayer for Discovering Your Purpose
Heavenly Father,

Thank You for the unique purpose You have for my life. Teach me to trust Your plans and to seek Your guidance as I discover and embrace the calling You have given me. Help me to use my gifts and experiences to glorify You and further Your kingdom. Thank You for filling my life with hope and for leading me every step of the way. Amen.

Day 14
Clarifying Your Vision

"Where there is no vision, the people perish: but he that keepeth the law, happy is he." — Proverbs 29:18

Vision is a gift from God, illuminating the path He has set before us. Proverbs 29:18 reminds us that without vision, we lose direction and purpose, making us vulnerable to distractions, uncertainty, and feelings of being lost. A clear vision aligns our hearts with God's plans, allowing us to move forward with confidence and focus.

Clarifying your vision begins with seeking God's guidance. Are there areas in your life where your goals or dreams feel unclear or disconnected from His will? Sometimes, we pursue things out of personal desire or societal expectations rather than seeking God's purpose. When we bring these goals before Him, He refines them, aligning them with His perfect plans for our lives.

Today, reflect on your vision. Where do you feel misaligned or unsure? Ask God to provide clarity and to reveal the steps He wants you to take. Trust that as you seek His will, He will illuminate your path and give you the confidence to move forward in alignment with His purpose.

Intention Setting
Today, focus on clarifying your vision:
 1. Reflect on areas where your vision feels unclear or misaligned, and bring them to God in prayer.
 2. Seek God's guidance by meditating on Proverbs 29:18 and trusting Him to reveal His purpose for your life.
 3. Take one intentional step to align your actions with the vision God is showing you.

Gratitude Focus
Today, reflect on God's goodness in:
 1. The clarity He provides when you seek Him.
 2. The gifts and talents He has given you to fulfill His purpose.
 3. The assurance that His vision for your life is good and filled with hope.

Action Plan
Take practical steps to clarify your vision and align with God's purpose:
 1. Spend 15 minutes in prayer asking God to reveal His vision for your life. Write down any thoughts or insights that come to mind.
 2. Identify one goal or dream that feels misaligned and ask God to refine it or replace it with His purpose.
 3. Reflect at the end of the day on how seeking God's vision brought clarity, peace, or new direction.

Prayer for Clarifying Your Vision
Heavenly Father,

Thank You for the vision You have for my life—a vision filled with hope, purpose, and Your glory. Help me to align my desires and actions with Your plans. Where my vision is unclear, provide clarity. Where my goals are misaligned, refine them to reflect Your will. Teach me to trust in Your guidance and to walk boldly in the direction You reveal. Fill my heart with peace and confidence as I seek Your purpose. Amen.

Week 2 Reflection

1. What new insights about yourself or your journey did you gain this week?

2. How has God shown His presence in your life during this week?

3. What progress have you made in aligning your life with God's vision?

4. How has your understanding of faith and resilience deepened?

Week 2 Assessment

1. What areas of your life are becoming clearer as you progress?

2. What habits or practices have strengthened your connection with God?

3. What goals or intentions will guide your final week of transformation?

4. How can you continue to trust God's timing and guidance?

DAY 15
Replacing Desperation with Devotion

But seek first the kingdom of God and His righteousness, and all these things will be added to you. — Matthew 6:33

Desperation often arises when life feels uncertain or out of control. The pressures of the world—deadlines, expectations, financial struggles, or relationships—can push us to take matters into our own hands. We convince ourselves that striving harder, planning more, or worrying endlessly will somehow create the solutions we desperately seek. But this path only leads to exhaustion, frustration, and a growing sense of anxiety.

Matthew 6:33 reminds us of a better way. Instead of frantically trying to piece life together on our own, God calls us to seek Him first. When we prioritize devotion to His kingdom and righteousness, He promises to meet our needs in His perfect timing. Desperation comes from fear and control; devotion flows from trust and surrender.

Think of a child in a storm. A child doesn't fight the storm—they instinctively run to their parent for safety. In the same way, God invites us to bring our worries, uncertainties, and fears to Him. Devotion isn't passive; it's an active choice to seek God through prayer, His Word, and aligning our actions with His will.

Reflect on the pressures you feel to "fix" or control certain areas of your life. Are you striving out of desperation, or are you trusting in God's provision? Replacing desperation with devotion means stepping out of the chaos and into His peace, knowing that He holds every detail of your life in His hands.

Let God guide your heart toward devotion today, reminding you that true peace and provision come not from striving, but from seeking Him first.

Intention Setting
Today, focus on replacing desperation with devotion:
 1. Reflect on an area where you feel desperate or out of control, and surrender it to God in prayer.
 2. Meditate on Matthew 6:33, asking God to help you seek His kingdom first in all things.
 3. Commit to one action today that demonstrates your devotion to God rather than striving for control.

Gratitude Focus
Today, reflect on God's goodness in:
 1. His faithfulness to provide for your needs.
 2. The peace that comes from trusting in His timing.
 3. His kingdom's eternal promises, which are greater than your worries.

Action Plan
Take practical steps to replace desperation with devotion:
 1. Spend time in prayer, surrendering one specific worry or area of striving to God.
 2. Choose one way to prioritize God's kingdom today, such as helping someone in need or dedicating time to worship.
 3. Reflect at the end of the day on how trusting God brought peace and a renewed sense of devotion.

Prayer for Replacing Desperation with Devotion
Heavenly Father,

Thank You for being my provider and my source of peace. Teach me to seek Your kingdom first and to trust in Your timing for all things. Replace my desperation with a heart devoted to You, and help me to rely on Your guidance instead of my own strength. Thank You for Your faithfulness, Your provision, and the peace that comes from knowing You are in control. Amen.

Day 16
Building Confidence in Your Path

The Lord is my light and my salvation; whom shall I fear? The Lord is the stronghold of my life; of whom shall I be afraid? — Psalm 27:1

Confidence comes from knowing that God is with us—guiding, protecting, and equipping us for the journey ahead. Yet, in a world that often measures confidence by appearances, achievements, or external validation, it can be easy to feel inadequate or unsure of our path. Psalm 27:1 provides a profound truth: our confidence doesn't come from who we are, but from who God is. He is our light in dark times, our salvation in trouble, and our stronghold in moments of weakness.

Building confidence in your path begins with trusting in God's plan. It requires acknowledging that while we may not see every step clearly, God sees the beginning, the middle, and the end of our journey. His guidance is perfect, His protection unwavering, and His provision abundant. Confidence in God allows us to move forward boldly, knowing that even if challenges arise, He is with us every step of the way.

Consider the areas in your life where you feel uncertain, hesitant, or even fearful. Is it a new opportunity, a difficult decision, or an unexpected season of change? Confidence doesn't mean the absence of challenges; it means trusting that God is greater than those challenges. When you align your path with His will and step forward in faith, He will strengthen your resolve and make your steps firm.

Today, ask God to reveal His strength in your areas of uncertainty. Let go of fear, lean into His promises, and choose to walk boldly in the path He has set before you. With God as your stronghold, you have every reason to be confident.

Intention Setting
Today, focus on building confidence in your path:
1. Reflect on one area where you feel uncertain or hesitant, and commit it to God in prayer.
2. Meditate on Psalm 27:1, reminding yourself that God is your stronghold and salvation.
3. Take one bold step forward in faith today, trusting that God is guiding and protecting you.

Gratitude Focus
Today, reflect on God's goodness in:
1. The confidence He provides through His presence and guidance.
2. The protection He offers during uncertain or challenging times.
3. The strength He gives you to take bold steps in faith.

Action Plan
Take practical steps to build confidence in your path:
1. Write down one specific fear or hesitation and surrender it to God in prayer.
2. Identify one small, faith-filled action to move forward in an area where you feel uncertain.
3. Reflect at the end of the day on how trusting in God's guidance gave you courage and clarity.

Prayer for Building Confidence in Your Path
Heavenly Father,

Thank You for being my light, my salvation, and my stronghold. Help me to trust in Your plan for my life and to walk boldly in faith, knowing that You are always with me. Strengthen my confidence in Your guidance and remove any fear or doubt that hinders my steps. Teach me to rely on Your promises and to face each day with courage and hope. Thank You for leading me with love and unwavering faithfulness. Amen.

Day 17
Creating Sustainable Growth Habits

And let us not grow weary of doing good, for in due season we will reap, if we do not give up. – Galatians 6:9

True transformation is not a one-time event; it's a journey sustained by daily choices and habits that align with God's will. Galatians 6:9 encourages us to persevere in doing good, promising that our consistent efforts will yield a harvest in God's perfect timing. This means that even when progress feels slow or unseen, we are called to remain faithful and trust that God is working through our actions.

Sustainable growth habits are not built overnight. They are the result of intentional, consistent actions that reflect God's purpose. Whether it's dedicating time to prayer, studying Scripture, serving others, or practicing gratitude, these small, daily commitments shape the foundation of a life aligned with God.

Reflect on the habits that have drawn you closer to God. Are there practices you've let slip or new habits you feel called to develop? Sustainable growth is about progress, not perfection. It's about showing up each day with a willing heart and trusting that God will meet you in your efforts.

Today, identify one habit that has strengthened your faith and one new habit you want to cultivate. Trust that with God's guidance, your small, consistent actions will lead to lasting transformation.

Intention Setting
Today, focus on creating sustainable growth habits:
1. Reflect on one habit that has strengthened your relationship with God and commit to continuing it.
2. Identify one new habit you'd like to develop that aligns with God's will.
3. Take one small step today to establish or reinforce a sustainable growth habit.

Gratitude Focus
Today, reflect on God's goodness in:
1. The growth He has already brought into your life through your efforts.
2. The opportunities He provides each day to align your habits with His purpose.
3. His promise to bless your perseverance and faithfulness.

Action Plan
Take practical steps to create sustainable growth habits:
1. Write down one small, consistent habit you can commit to for the next week (e.g., morning prayer, journaling, or a gratitude practice).
2. Remove one distraction or obstacle that hinders your spiritual growth.
3. Reflect at the end of the day on how practicing or planning your new habit impacted your mindset or faith.

Prayer for Creating Sustainable Growth Habits
Heavenly Father,

Thank You for the growth You have brought into my life and for the habits that draw me closer to You. Teach me to persevere in doing good and to trust in the harvest You have promised. Help me to establish sustainable habits that reflect Your will and purpose. Guide my actions and strengthen my faith as I walk with You each day. Thank You for Your faithfulness and for shaping my life through small, consistent steps. Amen.

Day 18
Cultivating Faith-Based Resilience

Blessed is the man who remains steadfast under trial, for when he has stood the test he will receive the crown of life. — James 1:12

Faith-based resilience is the ability to remain steadfast and unwavering under the weight of life's trials. James 1:12 reminds us that enduring challenges with faith not only brings blessings but also eternal rewards. Resilience is not about avoiding difficulty; it's about trusting in God's strength to guide us through it.

When trials come, it's natural to feel overwhelmed or question your ability to persevere. But God's Word offers assurance: He is with you in every struggle, equipping you with the strength to endure and grow. Resilience is built by leaning on His promises, staying rooted in prayer, and viewing each challenge as an opportunity to deepen your faith.

Think of a recent trial you've faced. How did God sustain you during that season? Did He provide comfort, guidance, or unexpected blessings along the way? Cultivating resilience requires reflecting on His faithfulness in the past and trusting Him for the future.

Today, focus on ways to cultivate resilience by turning to God for strength. Trust that no trial is too great for His power, and know that with each challenge, He is preparing you for something greater.

Intention Setting
Today, focus on cultivating faith-based resilience:
1. Reflect on a recent trial and identify how God's presence sustained you through it.
2. Meditate on James 1:12, trusting in God's promise to bless those who endure.
3. Take one action today to lean on God's strength instead of your own during a challenge.

Gratitude Focus
Today, reflect on God's goodness in:
1. The strength He provides during trials.
2. The lessons and growth that come through challenges.
3. His promise of eternal rewards for steadfast faith.

Action Plan
Take practical steps to cultivate resilience:
1. Identify one current challenge and write a prayer asking God for strength and guidance.
2. Find one Scripture that speaks to endurance and reflect on how it applies to your situation.
3. Reflect at the end of the day on how leaning on God's strength helped you face today's challenges.

Prayer for Cultivating Faith-Based Resilience
Heavenly Father,

Thank You for being my source of strength and hope during trials. Teach me to trust in Your promises and to remain steadfast in my faith, no matter the circumstances. Help me to see challenges as opportunities to grow closer to You and to rely on Your guidance every step of the way. Thank You for Your faithfulness and for the assurance that my endurance is not in vain. Strengthen me to face each trial with courage and unwavering trust in You. Amen.

Day 19
Sharing Your Transformation with Others

You are the light of the world. A city set on a hill cannot be hidden. – Matthew 5:14

Transformation is a deeply personal journey, but it is also a gift meant to bless and inspire others. Matthew 5:14 reminds us that we are called to be lights in the world, reflecting God's love, truth, and power. When you share your story of growth and transformation, you demonstrate God's faithfulness and invite others to experience His grace for themselves.

Sharing your transformation requires confidence—not in your own ability but in God's work through you. Your story doesn't need to be perfect or polished to make an impact. In fact, it's often the moments of struggle and surrender that resonate most with others. As you share, trust that God will use your words and experiences to plant seeds of hope and faith in others' hearts.

Reflect on how your transformation has impacted your relationships, choices, and overall outlook on life. How has God's work in your life become evident to those around you? Sharing your journey can take many forms—through words, actions, encouragement, or simply living as an example of God's love.

Today, ask God to give you the confidence to share your story, trusting Him to use it for His glory. Remember, your light is not meant to be hidden but to shine brightly, guiding others to the One who transforms lives.

Intention Setting
Today, focus on sharing your transformation with others:
 1. Reflect on one way your growth has positively impacted those around you.
 2. Identify someone in your life who could benefit from hearing your story of transformation.
 3. Ask God for the confidence to share your testimony and the wisdom to do it with grace and love.

Gratitude Focus
Today, reflect on God's goodness in:
 1. The ways He has used your transformation to bless others.
 2. The opportunities He provides to share His love and truth.
 3. The confidence He gives you to be a light in the world.

Action Plan
Take practical steps to share your transformation with others:
 1. Write down one specific example of how God has transformed your life.
 2. Identify one action—such as a conversation, encouragement, or act of kindness—that reflects God's work in you.
 3. Reflect at the end of the day on how sharing your transformation encouraged or inspired someone else.

Prayer for Sharing Your Transformation with Others
Heavenly Father,

Thank You for the transformation You have worked in my life. Help me to confidently share my story, trusting that You will use it to inspire others and bring glory to Your name. Teach me to reflect Your love and truth in all that I do, and give me the courage to be a light in the lives of those around me. Thank You for the opportunity to share Your goodness and for the ways You continue to work in and through me. Amen.

Day 20
Becoming a Light in Your Community

Let your light shine before others, so that they may see your good works and give glory to your Father who is in heaven. – Matthew 5:16

As you near the end of this transformative journey, it's time to fully embrace the call to reflect God's light in your community. Matthew 5:16 reminds us that our actions, character, and faith are powerful testimonies that can point others to God's glory. Being a light isn't just about what we say; it's about how we live.

Clarity and spiritual growth play a central role in becoming a light. Clarity comes from understanding your identity in Christ and His purpose for your life. When you grow spiritually, you become more aligned with God's will, allowing His love and truth to shine through you. This light isn't meant to glorify yourself—it's meant to draw others closer to Him.

Being a light in your community involves serving others, standing firm in faith, and living out God's love and grace. It's in the small, everyday actions—offering encouragement, showing kindness, and living with integrity—that others begin to see God at work in you.

Reflect on how God has equipped you to serve and inspire those around you. Where is your light most needed right now? Is there a specific person, group, or cause God is calling you to impact? Ask Him to guide you and give you the confidence to step into this role, trusting that even small acts of faith can have a lasting impact on His kingdom.

Intention Setting
Today, focus on becoming a light in your community:
1. Reflect on one way your spiritual growth has prepared you to serve others.
2. Identify a need in your community or circle where your light can shine brightly.
3. Commit to one action today that reflects God's love and truth to those around you.

Gratitude Focus
Today, reflect on God's goodness in:
1. The clarity He has given you about your purpose and role in His kingdom.
2. The opportunities He provides to impact others for His glory.
3. The growth and confidence He has built in you to shine His light.

Action Plan
Take practical steps to be a light in your community:
1. Pray for guidance on how and where God wants you to serve or encourage others.
2. Choose one specific action to bless someone in your community today—such as volunteering, offering encouragement, or simply listening with compassion.
3. Reflect at the end of the day on how being a light impacted both you and those around you.

Prayer for Becoming a Light in Your Community
Heavenly Father,

Thank You for the clarity and growth You have brought into my life. Help me to be a light that reflects Your love, truth, and grace to those around me. Show me where I am most needed and guide me in serving others with humility and faith. Give me the courage to stand firm in my faith and the confidence to shine brightly for Your glory. Thank You for using me to bring hope and inspiration to my community. Amen.

Day 21
Living a Life of Alignment and Purpose

I have fought the good fight, I have finished the race, I have kept the faith. — 2 Timothy 4:7

You have reached the final day of this transformative journey—a time to celebrate, reflect, and step boldly into the life God has prepared for you. Proverbs 16:3 reminds us that living a life of alignment and purpose begins with committing every aspect of our lives to the Lord. When we trust Him with our plans, He guides and establishes them in ways that reflect His glory and bring fulfillment to our souls.

Alignment with God means walking in harmony with His will, trusting His timing, and surrendering our desires to His greater purpose. Purpose is the outflow of this alignment—living intentionally, using your gifts to serve others, and reflecting His love in every area of your life. This doesn't mean life will be free of challenges, but it does mean that with God as your foundation, every step will be meaningful and directed.

Today is not an ending but a beginning. Commit to continuing the practices that have deepened your faith and strengthened your walk with God. Trust that He will lead you to live a life of alignment and purpose, one step at a time.

Intention Setting
Today, focus on living a life of alignment and purpose:
1. Celebrate the growth and transformation God has brought into your life.
2. Commit to continuing the habits and practices that align with His will.
3. Reflect on how you will stay intentional in your walk with God.

Gratitude Focus
Today, reflect on God's goodness in:
1. The transformation God has worked in your heart and mind.
2. The strength He has given you to persevere and grow.
3. His promise to guide you in the next steps of your journey.

Action Plan
Take practical steps to live a life of alignment and purpose:
1. Write a personal commitment to live a life of alignment and purpose.
2. Identify one habit or practice you will continue as part of your walk with God.
3. Reflect at the end of the day on how God has prepared you for this new chapter.

Prayer for Living a Life of Alignment and Purpose
Heavenly Father,

Thank You for guiding me through this journey of transformation. I praise You for the growth, clarity, and strength You have given me. Help me to live a life that reflects Your purpose, walking boldly in faith and serving others with love. Teach me to stay aligned with Your will and to trust You in every step of my journey. Thank You for being my guide, my strength, and my greatest joy. Amen.

A WORD FROM THE AUTHOR

Dear Devoted Seeker!

Congratulations on completing this 21-day journey of transformation! What a beautiful step you have taken to align your life with God's purpose, to deepen your faith, and to walk boldly in His will. My prayer for you is that these 21 days have inspired clarity, healing, and a renewed connection with the One who created you for a life of abundance and purpose.

The idea for this guide was born out of a desire to help individuals take their first steps toward a holistic life—one rooted in God's Word, built on faith, and sustained by intentional actions. As someone who has spent years helping others navigate the complexities of emotional, mental, and spiritual challenges, I know the power of transformation when it is guided by the truth of God's promises.

This guide is not an end but a beginning. You have laid the foundation for a life that reflects the fullness of God's grace, and I encourage you to continue building on this foundation. Seek His wisdom daily, commit to habits that honor Him, and trust His timing in every aspect of your journey.

I invite you to explore other resources I've created to support you in your walk with God. Each one is designed to help you deepen your relationship with Him while addressing the spiritual, emotional, and mental areas of life that are critical for living in alignment with His will.

Thank you for allowing me to be a part of your journey. I am celebrating with you and praying for your continued growth, peace, and purpose. May your life be a testimony of God's faithfulness and love, inspiring others to seek Him as you have.

With love and gratitude,
Jennifer Jackson Penick
Believer. Encourager. Member of the Body of Christ.

Author Bio

Jennifer is a devoted follower of Christ with a heart for helping others live fully aligned with God's Word. With a background in mental, behavioral, and emotional health, Jennifer has dedicated her work to guiding individuals toward holistic transformation. Her passion lies in creating resources that inspire clarity, healing, and intentional living, all rooted in the promises of God.

Made in the USA
Columbia, SC
24 December 2024

48557884R10031